This Journal
Belongs to

______________________________________

www.ingramcontent.com/pod-product-compliance
Lightning Source LLC
LaVergne TN
LVHW051242050326
832903LV00028B/2525
* 9 7 8 1 7 0 3 0 2 1 7 9 0 *